Contents

Happy Families	4
Nazis and Jews	7
Going Away	8
The Conquest of Holland	11
Into Hiding	12
The Occupation of Holla...	
Daily Routines	
Special Occasions	
The Progress of War	23
Betrayed!	24
Concentration Camps	27
Afterward	28
Find Out More …	30
Glossary	31
Index	32

©1989 Franklin Watts

Tames, Richard1.
   Anne Frank/Richard Tames
     p. cm — (Lifetimes)
   Bibliography: p.
   Includes index.
   ISBN 0-531-10763-9 (lib.)/ISBN 0-531-24608-6 (pbk.)
   1. Frank, Anne. 1929–1945 – Juvenile literature. 2. Holocaust.
Jewish (1939–1945) – Netherlands – Amsterdam – Biography – Juvenile
literature. 3. Jews – Netherlands – Amsterdam – Biography – Juvenile
literature. 4. Amsterdam (Netherlands) – Biography – Juvenile
literature. I. Title. II. Series: Lifetimes (London, England)
DS135.N6F736 1989
940.53'15'03924 – dc19
[B]

First published in the USA by
Franklin Watts Inc.
95 Madison Avenue
New York
N.Y. 10016

Phototypeset by: JB Type, Hove, East Sussex
Printed in: Belgium
Series Editor: Penny Horton
Designed by: Ross George
First Paperback Edition 1991

89-5350
CIP
AC

Happy Families

Most books about famous people only tell the reader about what the person was like as a child, to help explain what they were like as a grown-up. But this book is all about one particular person's childhood, because she never had a chance to grow up. Very few people become famous as children, but Anne Frank was one of those few.

To understand why Anne Frank became famous we must know something about her family background.

The Frank family settled in the German city of Frankfurt in the seventeenth century. As the city expanded and grew rich by trade, so the Frank family also prospered.

Otto Frank, Anne Frank's father, was born in 1889. His father, Anne's grandfather, was a successful banker and the family lived in a pleasant suburb of the city.

When Otto left school, he went to study art at the famous University of Heidelberg. However, when a friend offered him the chance to go to the United States, he left university at once and went to work in Macy's department store, New York. A year after Otto went to New York news reached him that his father had died. He went back to his family in Germany immediately and got a job in an engineering factory.

During World War I (1914–18) Otto and his two brothers served in the German army as did millions of other German citizens. Otto rose to

The Frank family around 1900. Otto sits at the front in a sailor suit.

ANNE FRANK

Richard Tames

To Joanne

Franklin Watts

New York • London • Sydney • Toronto

Above: **Brothers in war. Otto Frank** (right) **in uniform, 1916.**

Above right: **Otto and Edith Frank on honeymoon at San Remo.**

the rank of lieutenant. When the war ended he left the army and went to work for his father's banking firm.

In 1925 Otto married Edith Höllander and they decided to live in Frankfurt, where most of the Frank family had lived for so long. The following year Otto and Edith had their first child and called her Margot Betti. Their second daughter was born on June 12, 1929. They called her Annelies Marie – Anne, for short.

Because Germany was defeated in World War I, the 1920s were difficult times for the German people. They were angry about the past and worried about the future.

In 1929 prosperity in the United States suddenly collapsed. People rushed to take their savings out of banks. Factories went out of business and people lost their jobs. Because the United States was such a rich country all the other great trading countries that did business with the United States were affected too. As one of these trading countries Germany's problems became even worse.

In Frankfurt the output of the city's factories fell by two-thirds between 1929 and 1932. By 1932 more than 70,000 people were out of work in the city.

In 1933 Otto Frank was fortunate to still have a job and a nice house in a bright, modern suburb. Even so, he decided to leave his job, his home and his country, to take Edith and the two girls to live in Holland.

It was the year that Adolf Hitler and the Nazi Party came to power in Germany, and the Frank family were Jews.

Above: Hitler, as leader, addresses the German Reichstag (Parliament).

Below: **The ancient trading city of Frankfurt in West Germany.**

Nazis and Jews

The defeat of Germany in 1918 made many Germans confused and angry. One of these people was a soldier who was temporarily blinded from a gas attack. His name was Adolf Hitler.

Hitler had been born in German-speaking Austria. As a young man he developed some very strange ideas which he came to believe in very strongly:–

All human beings could be divided up into various races and that some of these races were better than others; the most superior group were a people Hitler called **"Aryan"** and that Aryans had invented most of the great advances in art and science throughout history; the German-speaking people were the best of all the Aryans and ought to be united together in one nation to rule the world; the inferior races of the world included **Slavs** (like Russians and Poles), black people and Jews. These people, he believed, ought to be enslaved for the benefit of Aryans and in the end ought to die out altogether.

Hitler blamed the Jews for Germany's defeat. He said they were too rich and successful and cared nothing for Germany. This ignored the fact that many Jews like Otto Frank also served loyally in the German army during World War I.

By 1919, Hitler had joined the National Socialist German Workers' Party – the Nazis and soon became its leader. He promised to make Germany the most powerful country in the world.

During the 1920s few Germans took any notice of the Nazis but as the country's problems worsened, more and more people began to listen to Hitler's ideas. In 1933 the Nazi Party became the most popular party in Germany and Hitler became head of government.

As soon as the Nazis were in power they began to treat the Jews like enemies. Many Jews decided to leave Germany before they lost more than their jobs. One of them was Otto Frank.

These photographs, published in a Nazi propaganda booklet, were meant to illustrate the difference between "Aryan" (above) **and "alien"** (below) **children.**

Going Away

Above: **German Jews queue outside a travel agent trying to find a passage to freedom.**

Left: **The bustling street market in Waterloo Square, Amsterdam, in the centre of the Jewish community of the city.**

Otto Frank knew that there was a large Jewish community in Amsterdam, Holland's biggest city. For hundreds of years Holland had welcomed refugees from other countries, even though it was a crowded country. They brought valuable new skills which helped to make Holland prosperous.

During World War I, Holland had been neutral and took no part in the fighting. Mr. Frank therefore believed that his family would be happy and safe there.

The Frank family took a house in the southern part of Amsterdam. Mr. Frank started up a new business which was a branch of a German company, selling foodstuffs.

The whole family had to learn to speak Dutch and Margot and Anne had to go to a new school. They soon learned to speak Dutch well and made plenty of new friends.

Mr. Frank's new business did very well. So much so that he had to hire new staff. Two of them became good friends of the family – Miep Gies, an Austrian girl who organized the office work, and Mr. van Daan, who was an expert on spices.

But Mr. Frank was still worried by the news from Germany, where the Nazis were steadily making life worse for the Jews. In 1938 Mrs. Frank's two brothers escaped from Germany to the United States and her mother came to live in Holland. Britain and France prepared for war against Germany; but Holland expected to remain neutral.

Above: **Did you get enough to eat? Jewish refugee children in England.**

Below: **Anne** (arrowed, centre) **attends a modern Dutch school.**

Above: **Anne** (2nd left) **with friends on her tenth birthday.**

Meanwhile Margot and Anne made good progress at school. Margot liked studying and did brilliantly in her examinations. Anne liked taking part in plays and going to the movies.

In September 1939 Germany attacked Poland. This was the beginning of World War II. Poland was defeated in a few weeks. In Holland Mr Frank could do nothing but follow the news and attend to his work. In January 1940 the business moved to bigger premises – a large old building at 263 Prinsengracht.

In April 1940 Germany invaded Denmark and Norway. A month later Germany attacked France, Belgium, Luxembourg – and Holland.

Below: **Out of the sky, German paratroopers invade Holland. May 1940.**

The Conquest of Holland

The German invasion of Holland began on Friday May 10, 1940. It came as a complete shock to the Dutch people, who were not prepared for such an attack. They heard bombers droning overhead while it was still dark. When they got up in the morning they heard rumors that German troops had landed by parachute and seized key roads and bridges. During that day Queen Wilhelmina spoke on the radio and told her people that the Germans had indeed invaded Holland. Later radio announcements told everyone to be in their houses by eight o'clock and to black out their windows so that the bombers could not see their targets.

It soon became clear that the Dutch army, taken by surprise and outnumbered, could only hold out for a few days. Queen Wilhelmina and the government fled by ship to England. In a radio broadcast on May 14, a general of the Dutch army announced that the Germans had bombed the great port of Rotterdam, killing 900 people and destroying 24,000 houses and that to save further loss of life and property among civilians the Dutch army would surrender.

The Dutch people were stunned by the speed of the disaster. Only members of the Dutch Nazi Party (NSB) could look forward to the future.

Dutch troops surrender their arms at the Dutch seat of government.

Into Hiding

Above: **Mr. Koophuis shows the concealed entrance to the annex.**

Above left: **The Westerkerk, showing the Prinsengracht.**

The Nazis soon began making life miserable for the Jewish population in Holland. In October 1940, Otto Frank, like every other Jewish businessman, had to register his company with the German authorities. He knew that this meant that the Nazis were making a list of all Jewish businesses so that they could take them over. In June 1941, Mr. Frank, like all other Jews, had the letter "J" stamped on his identity card. In September, Margot and Anne were made to leave their school and go to a separate school for Jewish children. In the spring of 1942 all Jews were ordered to wear a yellow **Star of David** on their clothes so that they could be instantly recognized. Jews were forbidden to use public transportation or own bicycles so Mr. Frank had to walk all the way to and from his office.

Otto Frank feared that far worse was to come. As it was impossible for him to escape with a young family he decided that the only other way to stay safe was to disappear. He began to prepare a hiding place in the upstairs rooms of the Prinsengracht building. This meant fitting them out with furniture and facilities for washing and cooking, as well as storing a hoard of food – 150 cans of vegetables and 30 kgs (20 lbs) of dried peas and beans.

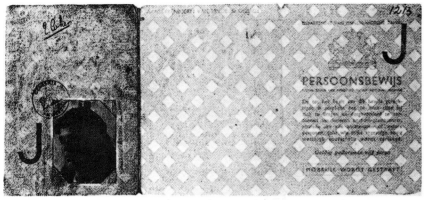

Left: **A personal identity card stamped with the letter J for Jew.**

Below: **A plan showing the interior of the secret annex.**

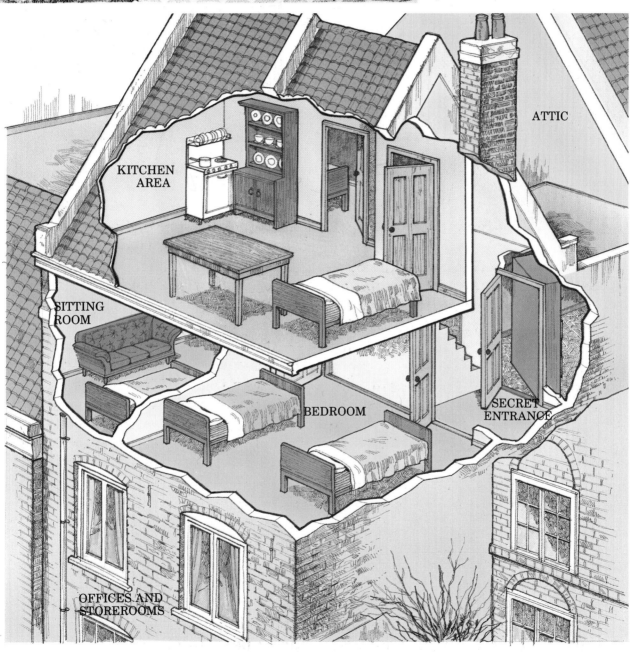

KITCHEN AREA

ATTIC

SITTING ROOM

BEDROOM

SECRET ENTRANCE

OFFICES AND STOREROOMS

In hiding: top row, left to right — **Otto, Edith, Anne and Margot Frank;** bottom row — **Mr. and Mrs. van Daan, Peter and Mr. Dussel. Thanks to Otto's quick thinking and forward planning, the family and their closest friends lived in safety for two years in the secret annex.**

In July 1942, a card came through the mail, addressed to Margot ordering her to report to a labor camp. From there it was likely that she would be sent to work in Germany.

Mr. Frank knew that if Margot went to the labor camp they might never see her again. There was no time for delay. Ready or not, he knew that they must move into their hiding place immediately. Everyone rushed to pack their belongings. Anne put her most precious things in her school satchel:—

"The first thing I put in was this diary, then hair-curlers, handkerchiefs, school books, a comb, old letters; I put in the craziest things ... But I'm not sorry, memories mean more to me than dresses."

At 7:30 in the morning on Monday July 6, 1942, the Frank family walked out of their home in the suburbs for the last time. They needed to carry as much as they could but had to be careful not to attract attention to themselves. Carrying a suitcase might mean being stopped and searched. So they wore as many clothes as they could:—

"We put on heaps of clothes as if we were going to the North Pole ... I had on two undershirts, three pairs of panties, a dress, on top of that a skirt, jacket, summer coat, two pairs of stockings, lace-up shoes, woolly cap, scarf and still more … ".

The Franks' "Secret Annex" consisted of just six rooms. For two years this was to be not just their home but the whole world for no less than eight people – Mr. and Mrs. Frank, Margot and Anne, Mr. and Mrs. van Daan and their son Peter, and Mr. Dussel, a dentist, who joined them in November 1942.

At first Anne enjoyed all the unpacking and settling-in jobs and wrote that it was "like being on holiday in a very peculiar boarding-house." She soon brightened up the room she shared with Margot by covering the walls with postcards and pictures of movie stars.

It was not long, however, before they began to get on each other's nerves. Mr. and Mrs. Frank couldn't stand the clock in the nearby church tower, which chimed every quarter of an hour, day and night. Anne became cross with Margot for coughing when she was trying to get to sleep. Mrs. van Daan was annoyed by Anne's non-stop chattering. And no one, of course, could go out.

However, other people could go in. And without their help in bringing food and warning of curious neighbors the annex dwellers could never have survived for more than a few days. These brave people were Mr. Frank's employees – Mr. Kraler and Mr. Koophuis, Elli Vossen, Miep Gies and her new husband, Jan. Although in her diary, Anne called Jan, Henk, to protect his identity.

From left to right:
Mr. Koophuis, Miep Gies, Elli Vossen and Mr. Kraler. These were the helpers who became a human lifeline for the annex dwellers.

The Occupation of Holland

In the autumn of 1940, **persecution** of the Jews began in earnest. Any Jew working for the government lost his job. In February 1941, four hundred Jewish men and boys were rounded up in Amsterdam and taken away. Thousands of Dutch people staged a three day strike in protest. But Dutch Nazis were eager to help the occupation forces and 30,000 members actually volunteered to fight for the Germans.

Gradually a Dutch **resistance** movement began to form. 30,000 people were involved in printing newsheets to spread truthful news about the war. 20,000 Dutch people helped to hide Jews and more than 200,000 went into hiding themselves rather than work for the Germans. Others forged official permits and passes. **Sabotage** groups blew up offices where records were kept. Many Dutch collaborators were assassinated and all the time the arrest and **deportation** of Jews went on until more than 115,000 had been forced to leave their homes. Most were taken to Westerbork, a specially-built camp in eastern Holland. Anne knew that Westerbork was bad and guessed that what followed was worse:–

"It is impossible to escape; most of the people in the camp are branded as inmates by their shaven heads. If it is as bad as this in Holland whatever will it be like in the distant and barbarous regions they are sent to? … The British radio speaks of their being gassed."

Left: **A Dutch Nazi killed by a member of the resistance for betraying his country.**

Daily Routines

Life in the annex soon settled down to a routine. An alarm clock rang at 6:45 am and everyone took their turn in the bathroom. By 8:30 the boys who worked in the warehouse on the ground floor had arrived and as they knew nothing about the hiding place it was essential to avoid making any noise while they were at work. So everyone had to be finished in the bathroom by 8:30 to avoid any sounds of running water.

Breakfast was served at 9:00. Like all other meals it was eaten in the van Daan's room, up on the top floor, where they were least likely to be heard. After breakfast had been cleared away all movement was kept to an absolute minimum. Shoes were forbidden. Anyone who moved around did so in their stockinged feet or wore slippers.

At 12:30 the warehouse boys went home for their lunch and it was possible to breathe more easily. By 1:00 the helpers from the office would come upstairs to listen to the BBC and have a cup of soup. By 2:00 in the afternoon everything had to be silent again. The helpers went back to work and the Franks and van Daans settled down to pass the afternoon sleeping or reading. Once the office had emptied at 5:30 everyone could move around again and the evening meal was prepared and served. In the evenings, there were household chores to be done and usually another broadcast to listen to from London.

DAILY ROUTINE

6.45am	Wake up. Take turns in bathroom
8.30am	Warehouse downstairs opens for work. SILENCE IN ANNEXE
9.00am	Breakfast in the Van Daan's room.
12.30pm	Warehouse closes for lunch.
1.00pm	Lunch with helpers from downstairs. Listen to BBC radio.
2.00pm	Warehouse re-opens. SILENCE IN ANNEXE Afternoon spent reading, sleeping or writing
5.30pm	Warehouse closes. Prepare and eat evening meal. Housework. Listen to BBC radio.
9.00pm	Preparations for going to bed. Move furniture, arrange bedding, take turns in bathroom.
12.30am	Everyone in bed.

Then, at 9:00 pm it was time to begin the preparations for going to bed. Most of the furniture had to be moved around so that beds could be arranged and bedding taken out of storage. Then, again, everyone took their turn in the bathroom, starting with Anne, the youngest, and ending with Mr. Dussel.

At weekends the routine varied, with no welcome visitors from downstairs and even more need to keep quiet to avoid attracting the slightest attention to what was supposed to be an empty building.

Feeding eight people was a major headache. Using forged ration cards, acquired through the resistance, Miep Gies went shopping for fresh food every weekday. A friendly greengrocer and butcher allowed her to buy far more than she could ever have needed for herself and her husband. They knew that something strange was going on but were wise enough not to ask any questions. The greengrocer even delivered heavy sacks of potatoes to the Prinsengracht office to save Miep the trouble and possible danger of wheeling them through the streets on her bicycle.

Preparing food helped to pass the time. Mrs. van Daan was a very good cook and both Anne and Margot willingly helped with chores like cleaning vegetables. Mr. van Daan was an expert on spices, so he was able to make sausages, which could be stored for an emergency as well

Weekly, on the eve of the Sabbath, a Jewish family pauses to celebrate the security of being together.

BREAKFAST:

Dry bread and coffee

LUNCH:

Soup or porridge, and bread

DINNER:

Spinach and lettuce with potatoes (described in the diary as 20cms long and rotten); fried potatoes occasionally with vegetable or lettuce. Special treat: sausages.

as making a tasty treat. Peter's job was to haul the potatoes and other heavy shopping up from the ground floor to the attic. Leftovers and trash could not be put out for fear of drawing attention to what was supposed to be an uninhabited office building. So every kind of waste had to be burned in the stove – even in the hottest weather. Being inventive and well-organized the inhabitants of the annex usually had enough to eat. But this often meant eating the same food again and again.

In March, 1943 Anne complained about this in her diary:–

"We have eaten so many kidney beans and haricot beans that I can't bear the sight of them any more. The mere thought of them makes me feel quite sick."

A month later it was even worse:–

"Our food is miserable. Dry bread and coffee substitute for breakfast. Dinner: spinach or lettuce for a fortnight on end. Potatoes twenty centimetres long and tasting sweet and rotten. Whoever wants to follow a slimming course should stay in the 'Secret Annex'".

In May 1944 the friendly greengrocer was arrested for hiding two Jews in his house. Anne knew that these hard times would get harder:–

"Mommy says we shall cut out breakfast altogether, have porridge and bread for lunch, and for supper fried potatoes and possibly once or twice a week vegetables or lettuce, nothing more. We're going to be hungry, but anything is better than being discovered."

Outside the secret annex, World War II continued to take lives and destroy towns and cities. When the Nazis bombed Rotterdam, the city lost 24,000 buildings and 900 lives.

Anne and Margot missed going to school and seeing all their friends. But they kept on studying just the same. Mr. Frank acted as their teacher and was determined that they should not fall behind. Anne needed little encouragement. She wanted to be a writer and knew that a good education was essential.

Anne's hobbies also had to be quiet ones. Keeping her diary and writing stories took up a lot of her time, but most of the long, empty hours were spent reading. The tales of the ancient Greek gods were her favo-rite subjects. She also liked reading movie magazines and cutting out the pictures of movie stars to put on her bedroom wall. Exercise was, of course, a major problem for every-one. But it was possible to do fitness routines, even in the dark. And Anne practiced ballet steps, even making herself a ballet dress to practice in.

However, trying to keep busy did not always work. In October 1943 Anne confessed to her diary:–

"My nerves often get the better of me: it is especially on Sundays that I feel rotten … I wander from one room to another, downstairs and up again, feeling like a songbird … beating itself in utter darkness against the bars of its cage … I go and lie on the divan and sleep, to make the time pass more quickly, and the stillness and the terrible fear, because there is no way of kill-ing them."

Of course, Anne realized that she was not the only one who felt down-hearted at times and made a record of everyone else's dearest wish if they could go outside:–

"Margot and Mr. van Daan long more than anything for a hot bath filled to overflowing and want to stay in it for half an hour. Mrs. van Daan wants most to go and eat cream cakes immediately. Dussel thinks of nothing but seeing Lotje, his wife; Mommy of her cup of coffee; Daddy is going to visit Mr. Vossen first; Peter the town and a theater, while I should find it so blissful, I shouldn't know where to start!"

Special Occasions

Some days *were* different. Despite all their difficulties the prisoners of the annex tried hard to celebrate days that were special for individuals or for everyone. On Peter's sixteenth birthday he received a game of Monopoly, and, to show that he had grown up, a razor and a cigarette lighter. On her birthday, Mrs. van Daan got a pot of jam and coupons for cheese, meat and bread and on Anne's fifteenth birthday:—

"All five parts of Sprenger's *History of Art*, a set of underwear, a handkerchief, two bottles of yogurt, a pot of jam, a spiced gingerbread cake, and a book on **botany** from Mommy and Daddy, a double bracelet from Margot, a book from the van Daans, sweet peas from Dussel, candy and exercise books from Miep and Elli and, the high spot of all, the book *Maria Theresa* and three slices of full-cream cheese from Kraler. A lovely bunch of peonies from Peter; the poor boy took a lot of trouble to try and find something, but didn't have any luck."

There were holidays, too. In December 1942 the annex celebrated both Chanukah, the Jewish festival of lights, and St. Nicholas Day, a Dutch national festival for children. Anne was given a doll, whose skirt could be used as a bag.

The following year they celebrated

A child celebrates Chanukah, the Jewish festival of lights.

Christmas:—

"On Friday evening for the first time in my life I received something for Christmas ... Miep had made a

lovely Christmas cake, on which was written 'Peace 1944.' Elli had provided a pound of biscuits of pre-war quality. For Peter, Margot and me a bottle of yogurt, and a bottle of beer for each of the grown-ups. Everything was so nicely done up and there were pictures stuck on the different parcels."

Terrified of making a noise that might attract attention, the inhabitants of the annex were liable to jump at any sudden or unusual noise they heard. One night Mrs. van Daan was sure she heard burglars. It turned out to be a pack of enormous rats. Four months later, in July 1943, Anne recorded excitedly in her diary:–

"Burglars again, but real this time! … They stole two cash boxes … money-orders and check books and then, worst of all, all the coupons for 150 kilos of sugar."

There was another burglary in March 1944. Anne realized that theft had become a disease:–

"… doctors are unable to visit the sick, because if they turn their backs on their cars for a moment, they are stolen; burglaries and thefts abound, so much so that you wonder what has taken hold of the Dutch for them suddenly to have become such thieves. Little children of eight and eleven years break the windows of people's homes and steal whatever they can lay their hands on. No one dares to leave his house unoccupied for five minutes, because if you go, your things go too."

A month later there was yet another burglary. The four men went downstairs. The four women waited upstairs. Mr. van Daan tried a bold bluff and shouted "Police!" The burglars ran away. The men came back upstairs. Then everyone heard another noise downstairs. This time it *was* the Dutch police, who had come to investigate the break-in. They came and they went. The prisoners of the annex breathed easily again.

The presents, given and received by the inhabitants of the annex for Christmas, 1943.

The Progress of War

Between the autumn of 1939, when the war began, and the summer of 1942, when the Franks went into hiding, the armies of Nazi Germany and its allies seemed unbeatable. But in 1943 the tide at last began to turn in favor of Britain, the United States and their allies. Anne kept up with the news by listening to the radio and noted important events in her diary. In July 1943 she wrote:–

" … the British have landed in Sicily now and Daddy is once again hoping for a 'quick finish'."

A couple of weeks later Anne noted excitedly:–

" … wonderful news, such as we have not heard for months, perhaps in all the war years. Mussolini has resigned … We jumped for joy … the suspense over Italy will awaken the hope that it will soon end, perhaps even this year."

On June 6, 1944 she was at last able to record:–

" 'This is **D-Day**' came the announcement over the British radio and quite rightly 'This is *the* day.' The invasion has begun! … the best part of the invasion is that I have the feeling that friends are approaching."

Southern Holland was liberated in September 1944 but the rest of the country had to wait until April 1945. During that hard winter over 20,000 Dutch people died of starvation.

Invasion. US troops and landing craft. Normandy, 1944.

Betrayed!

Friday August 4, 1944, began much like any other day in the secret annex. Miep Gies came up to collect the daily shopping list and Anne, as usual, bombarded her with chatter and questions. Miep was too busy in the office downstairs to stop and chat but promised to do so in the afternoon. She never got the chance.

In the middle of the morning a man in a raincoat walked into the office – pointing a revolver. He was a Dutch Nazi. Soon he was joined by other men – German Nazis and police. The people in the office heard them searching the building. After a couple of hours they could hear the footsteps of the people in the annex as they were pushed down the stairs

Above: **German troops raid homes and round up Jews in hiding.**

Left: **The attic in the annex where Anne wrote most of her diary.**

into the street and then into a German police truck.

Three days later Miep Gies went to the **Gestapo** headquarters in Amsterdam and tried to bribe the Nazi official who had arrested the Franks and van Daans. He might have been willing to let them go in return for money but was afraid of his superiors. Miep could do nothing more. A few days afterward a removal van came to the Prinsengracht offices. All the furniture and personal possessions left in the secret annex were taken away.

No one ever discovered who betrayed the inhabitants of the secret annex. Police records later showed that a payment of sixty Dutch guilders was made to an informant in respect of the raid on 263 Prinsengracht, but the informant remained nameless. There were Dutch Nazis living in a house across the garden behind the Prinsengracht office building. It may even have been one of the thieves who tried to burgle the offices from time to time.

The Franks, the van Daans and Mr. Dussel were taken to Westerbork. Mr. Dussel was taken to Neuengamme concentration camp where he died. The Franks and van Daans were loaded on to the last train to Auschwitz, the most well-known and feared of the concentration camps.

Above: **Dutch Jews waiting to be transported to Westerbork camp.**

Below: **The final departure. Dutch Jews leaving Westerbork for Auschwitz.**

At Auschwitz Mr. van Daan was gassed to death. Mr. Frank saw him being taken to the gas chambers. Mrs. Frank was so weak and ill that she died shortly before the camp was liberated by the Russians. Peter van Daan, at that point, was still fit enough to be herded away by the Schutzstaffel, or Secret Service (SS) who took a group of prisoners with them when they discovered that the Russians were approaching. Peter died in Mauthausen concentration camp on the day it was liberated by the Americans.

Mr. Frank survived his ordeal in Auschwitz, and when the Russians freed the camp, he made his way to Amsterdam, arriving at 263 Prinsengracht on June 3, 1945.

As soon as the Russians had chased the Nazis out of Auschwitz,

Arrival at Auschwitz. One queue for workers, one for death victims.

Mr. Frank had gone into the women's section to find out what had happened to his wife and daughters. Here he learned that his wife had just died and that Margot and Anne, together with Mrs. van Daan, had been taken to Bergen-Belsen. This gave Mr. Frank some hope that they might still be alive. Bergen-Belsen was a work camp rather than a death camp. There was cruelty and hunger and disease; but there were no gas chambers.

Mrs. van Daan died in Bergen-Belsen. Between February and March 1945 Margot caught typhus and died. Anne was now completely alone. Shortly afterward she, too, died of typhus.

Concentration Camps

A gas chamber at Majdanek destruction camp.

Within a few weeks of taking power in Germany in 1933, the Nazis set up the first "concentration camps." These were supposed to be tough prisons where criminals would be "re-educated." By 1939 there were three such camps in Germany and Austria, and another three in Poland, holding 21,000 prisoners.

After the outbreak of World War II the Nazis went beyond destroying rebellious individuals and began to wipe out whole groups of people that they considered "racially inferior." In the course of 1942, Nazi leaders began to plan "the final solution of the Jewish question" – the murder of eleven million Jews.

Some of the concentration camps became **extermination** camps, where the inmates were either worked to death or murdered on arrival. Most were killed in the gas chambers. Herded together, their clothes removed, they were driven into specially-built chambers where they were robbed not only of their possessions but even of their eyeglasses and gold fillings. In all, more than eight million people were murdered in the 2,000 Nazi concentration camps. Six million of them were Jews.

Afterward

In March 1944, Anne Frank listened to the Dutch news program from London and heard the broadcaster say that after the war the Dutch people ought to make a national collection of diaries and letters to record what they had been through. Anne put her own immediate thoughts down in her diary:–

"Just imagine how interesting it would be if I were to publish a romance of the 'Secret Annex.' The title alone would be enough to make people think it was a detective story."

Right: **Fame too late. The cover of the first edition of Anne's diary.**

Below: **Pages from Anne's diary.**

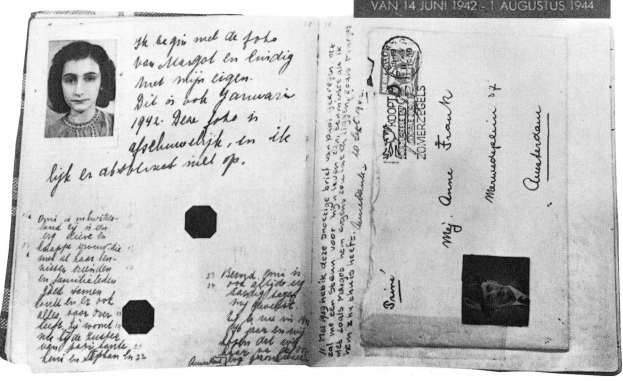

A few days later she returned to the subject of writing, showing how much it meant to her:–

"I can shake off everything if I write; my sorrows disappear, my courage is reborn. But, and that is the great question, will I ever be able to write anything great, will I ever become a journalist or a writer? I hope so, I hope so very much."

A month later Anne announced:–

"I want to publish a book entitled *Het Achterhuis* (*The Annex*) after the war. Whether I shall succeed or not, I cannot say, but my diary will be a great help."

The fact that Anne's diary survived at all was due to the quick thinking of Miep Gies. When Otto Frank returned from Auschwitz in June 1945, Miep Gies handed the manuscript of Anne's diary over to him. Mr. Frank translated some pages from the diary into German, so that his mother, who lived in Switzerland, could read it.

One day in 1947 Mr. Frank happened to mention the diary to a Jewish friend. When he asked to read it Mr. Frank gave him copies of some of the sections he had translated for his mother. The man then asked to read the whole diary. He was very impressed and showed it to a well-known historian, who wrote a newspaper article about it and said it ought to be published so that everyone could read it. It was published as *Het Achterhuis*, the title that Anne herself had chosen.

The first edition of Anne's diary soon sold out. So did a second. Foreign translations were made. The book was then turned into a play, which had its first Amsterdam performance in 1956. In 1959 it became the subject of a film, which was given a royal première.

In 1957 the house at 263 Prinsengracht became a museum, run by the Anne Frank Foundation, which exists to fight **racism** and **fascism** through education.

Anne Frank's diary has appeared in more than 50 different editions and sold more than 18 million copies. Anne wanted to grow up to be a writer. She never had the chance. Anne wanted to live after her death through her writing. She has.

A rear view of the Prinsengracht building — the secret annex.

Find Out More ...

Important Books

Anne Frank: The Diary of a Young Girl
There are many editions. Probably the most popular is the Penguin paperback edition first issued in 1968

The Diary of Anne Frank
Based on the Diary, this version was written by F. Goodrich and A. Hackett and edited by M. Marland. (Random House 1956)

Tales from the Secret Annexe
This is a collection of some of the stories Anne wrote while she was in hiding (Doubleday 1984) (Translated by R. Manheim and M. Mok)

Anne Frank in the World
This is an illustrated account of Anne's life and of events in Germany and Holland during her lifetime. Published by the Anne Frank Foundation (Anne Frank Stichting 1985)

Anne Frank Remembered: This is the story of Miep Gies. Who Helped to hide the Frank Family. Written by Miep Gies with Alison Leslie Gold (Simon & Schuster 1987)

Nazi Germany
This is a volume in the *Living Through History* series which shows how the history of Nazi Germany was experienced by fourteen people who lived during that period. Written by Richard Tames (Batsford 1985)

Germany
This account, written by Robert Gibson and Jon Nichol, describes the history of Germany from 1900 to the present. (Basil Blackwell 1985)

The Second World War
This is a brief illustrated survey of World War II, written by Charles Messenger (Watts 1986)

Important Addresses

Anne Frank Foundation
Keipeizersgracht 192
1016 DW
Amsterdam
Holland

Anne Frank Museum
Prinsengracht 263
1016 GV
Amsterdam
Holland

Glossary

Aryan   In Nazi belief, any person who was descended from caucasian Indo-European roots and of non-Jewish descent.

Botany   The science of plants, flowers and trees.

Deportation   The act of forcing someone to leave a country.

D-Day   June 6, 1944, when the Allies invaded Europe to free conquered countries from Nazi rule and end the war.

Extermination   An act of complete destruction.

Fascism   A political movement opposed to democracy and communism introduced by Benito Mussolini in Italy (1922–43).

Gestapo   The name for the German secret police under the Nazis.

Occupation   The takeover of control of a country by a foreign military power.

Persecution   To mistreat, oppress and constantly harass a race or religion.

Racism   Abusive or aggressive behavior toward people of a particular race based on the belief that they are inferior to the attackers' race.

Resistance   An organization fighting for national freedom in a country which has been occupied by enemy forces.

Sabotage   To deliberately damage or destroy.

Slavs   Peoples from East Europe or Russia who speak a similar language. These include Bulgarians, Russians, Poles and Czechs.

Star of David   A star with six points which is a symbol of the Jewish religion.

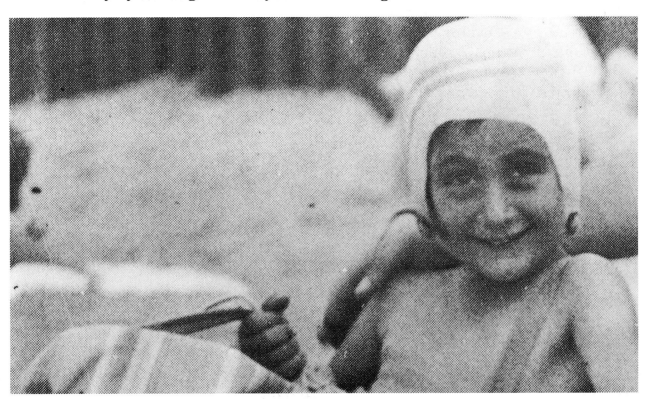

Index

Anne Frank Foundation 29
annex 13,14,15,17,19,21,22,24,25,28,29
   birthdays 21
   festivals 21–2
   food 12,17,18,19
   meals 17,19
   routines 17,18,19
Aryans 7
Austria 7,9,27

Belgium 10
Britain 9,11,23
   London 17,28

concentration camps 27
   Auschwitz 25,26,29
   Mauthausen 26
   Neuengamme 25

van Daan, Mr. 9,15,17,18,20,21,22,24,25,26
van Daan, Mrs. 15,17,18,20,21,22,24,25,26
van Daan, Peter 15,17,19,20,21,22,24,25,26
Denmark 10
diary 14,15,16,19,20,22,23,28,29
Dussel, Mr. 15,18,19,20,21,25
Dutch Nazi Party 11,16,24,25

France 9,10
Frank, Anne 9,12,14,15,20,22,24,26,28,29
   birth 5
   school 9,10,20
   friends 9,10
   hobbies 20
   birthdays 21
   typhus 26
   death 26
   fame 4,29
Frank, Edith 9,20,21,26
Frank family 4,5,6,8,9,14,15,17,23,24,25
Frank, Margot 9,10,12,14,20,21,22,26
Frank, Otto 4–5,6,7,8,9,10,12,14,20,21,26,29
Frankfurt 4,5,6

gas chambers 26,27
Germany 4,5,6,7,9,10,14,23,27
Gestapo 24
Gies, Miep 15,18,21,24,29
   Jan (Henk) 15

Hitler, Adolf 6,7
   beliefs 7
Holland 8,9,10,12,16,23
   Amsterdam 8,16,28
   invasion of 11
   occupation of 16
   Rotterdam 11
   starvation in 23
Hollander, Edith 5,6

Jews 6,7,12,16,19,27
   deportation of 16
   destruction of 27
   identity cards 12,13
   in hiding 16,19
   persecution of 7,9,12,16
   Star of David 12

Koophuis, Mr. 15
Kraler, Mr. 15,21

labour camps 14
   Bergen-Belsen 26
   Westerbork 16,25
Luxembourg 10

Nazis 7,9,12,16,23,24,26,27
Norway 10

Poland 10,27
Prinsengracht, 263 10,12,18,24,25,26,29

refugees 8,9
Resistance 16,18
Russia 26

Secret Service (SS) 26
Switzerland 29

United States 9,23,26
   New York 4

Vossen, Elli 15,21,22

Wilhelmina, Queen 11
World War I 4,5,7,8
World War II 10,27
   D-Day 23

Picture Acknowledgements

The publishers would like to thank the following for their kind permission to reproduce their photographs in this book:
The Anne Frank Foundation, Amsterdam frontispiece, 4,5 (left & right), 9 (bottom), 10 (top), 12 (left & right), 14,15,24 (bottom), 28 (top & bottom), 29,32; Gemeenteerchief, Amsterdam 8 (bottom); Gemeenteerchief, The Hague 11; Historiches Museum, Frankfurt 6; Rijksinstituut voor Oorlogsdocumentatie, Amsterdam 6 (top), 10 (bottom), 13 (top), 16,20,23,24 (top), 25 (top & bottom), 26,27. Photographer: Paul Seheult.
The following photographs were supplied by: BBC Hulton 9 (top), 18; Franklin Watts 21.
All the illustrations were supplied by Peter Bull.